ARIANNA,

THANK YOU SO .

FOR SHARING SACRED

SPACE WITH ME!

♥ KATE

little waves

A Tiny Memoir

KATE PELLETIER

Dedicated to Unconditional Love

Contents

Preface ix

1. Special 1

2. Frozen 3

3. Broken 5

4. Scarred 9

5. Dying 11

6. Trying 13

Acknowledgments 15

About the Author 17

Preface

These words were first shared at an event known as "Confluencia," a spoken-word night held at Naugatuck Valley Community College, located in Waterbury, Connecticut in the fall of 2017. When Steve Parlato, my colleague and the host of the event, asked me to consider reading, I said "No!" Then I said "Maybe?" Then I said "Yes," but the truth is, I knew I had to do it from the moment he asked me because it gave me that scary-in-a-good-way feeling.

At the time of the reading, I had no idea as to a common theme among my pieces. They appear here in the exact same order as I read them that night: chronologically. I have since come to recognize what now appears glaringly obvious. Their shared thread is sacred space. Sometimes it was held for me; sometimes it was not. There have been times when I have tried to hold it for myself, and times when I have attempted to hold it for others.

As you read these stories, you will inevitably begin to see aspects of yourself and your own experiences. In service of that, I have added reflections at the end of each section to support you in creating your own space for discovery and healing. Do them as you feel called to; let them go when they do not resonate.

1

Special

You're the shyest flower girl. You get to wear a big shiny white polyester dress with puffy sleeves and have your hair French braided with a special zigzag part. You think the 20 year old bride with blonde hair, tanned skin, and green eyes is the most beautiful woman you've ever seen. You get to hold a little white plastic basket with red rose petals when you walk down the aisle.

You make a mistake at the reception, though. In your little five year old head, you think that it is your duty to catch the bouquet and unsurprisingly to everyone but you, you do not. You believe that you have let everyone down; you have ruined it. The reception is high on a hill overlooking the ocean and you start to cry and run away down the steep grassy slope. A nice lady finds you and lets you sit on her lap and look at her wedding rings and you feel special and safe again. You didn't mess it up. It's ok. You're ok.

Reflections

Who catches you when you think you've fallen?
How do they do it?

_____

_____

_____

_____

_____

_____

_____

When have you thought you lost your "special?"
Where did it go? How did you get it "back?"

_____

_____

_____

_____

_____

_____

_____

2

Frozen

The great idea is to catch your sister's hand from the sled before she hits the bottom. But you miscalculated how hard it would be for your little arm to reach out and grab her and she slides past you easily, flying over the retaining wall and smacking her back on the metal electrical box below. You go for help. Your mom rushes out to carry her inside. You're saying you're sorry a hundred times, trying to explain what the plan was but no one hears you. It's your fault. Your mom takes your sister inside and you stand there freezing in the snow covered street, hating yourself. You ruined it.

Reflections

What do you do when no one hears you?

_____

_____

_____

_____

_____

_____

_____

How do you warm your own heart?

_____

_____

_____

_____

_____

_____

_____

3

Broken

"Relax your shoulders, sink down into the strength of your legs." As the instructor guides me into Warrior II, a moment of quiet comes, just then the voice inside my head almost always questions "When will this be over?"

…

I have asked for the big "over" two times in my life thus far. The first came when a wave smashed my head against the floor of the ocean. My sense of direction was gone; I couldn't find the surface. For a few seconds, I struggled but finding no air, I spoke to the water, to God. "If this is the end, you can take me." The moment I surrendered, a hand yanked my head out of the water and I found myself in the world again.

The second time wasn't by chance; I prayed for my life to be over with all my might. I was 19 years old and I had reached my breaking point over something that started when I was eleven and in fifth grade. I had acne. Not like a zit here and there. Not like once in a while or once a week. Not like in the commercials where some poor teenager has to clear a zit before a party and then it all turns out A-OK, just in time. I had persistent, always painful tender blistering skin that looked raw and especially hideous in my dorm's fluorescently lit bathroom. I couldn't even wash my face when any of the other girls were in the bathroom. I waited until the dead of night and stared at my skin, obsessed over my skin, scrubbed, picked and tortured my skin. Nothing worked. The red lesions reached deep into the layers of flesh and each new scan with my fingers uncovered the unmistakable tenderness of more as yet unseen but soon to be new cysts which I knew from much experience would take days to come to the surface, spend many days at the surface, and then spend many days fading away from the surface. I winced when anyone said they couldn't go to a party because they had ONE pimple. I could only imagine what people who said that felt about me. And imagine I did, all the time.

I wouldn't allow anyone to touch my face, kiss me too roughly, get too close to me. They might mess up my carefully applied makeup and see the hideous monster underneath. Some days, the darker ones, I wondered what would happen if I just held a lighter really close to my skin, let the skin melt into a scar. Scar tissue might be more predictable, I reasoned, fantasized.

On this night, I was crying. Not softly whimpering like a child into my pillow, but racking, uncontrollable sobs. The kind you hear a mother make at a funeral for a kid who wasn't supposed to die yet. Guttural. Barely even human. This is how I came to God the night I prayed sincerely, earnestly to die.

"God

Please take my soul tonight. I can't do it anymore. I am broken. I don't know what else to do."

…

When I bring my awareness back to the room, the instructor is speaking once again. "Warrior is hard. It can feel like you're being torn in two, but you'll make it. Just breathe. It will be over soon."

Reflections

What made you feel broken? How did you
rediscover your wholeness?

_____

_____

_____

_____

_____

_____

_____

What does healing really mean?

_____

_____

_____

_____

_____

_____

_____

4

Scarred

As we leave the exam room, I whisper to my mom, "Did you hear that? He used the word tumor to scare me." During the beginning of the exam, the exam where a surgeon explained that I did indeed have cancer, he was careful to say lesion, area, tissue, which didn't sound so bad. Tumor, however, sounded scary.

I think of the gash on my mother's forehead, the reason she never not has bangs. With skin cancer, they almost always take more flesh than they need to, just to be safe. I don't want this to happen to me so I see three or four doctors before I find a surgeon I trust who says, "Since it is technically on your left breast, your insurance should cover the cost of Mohs surgery, which is far more precise than a typical excision." I know now, for certain, that for the rest of my life, part of me will be gone. I will have a scar over my heart. I'm only 26 years old.

Reflections

What has scarred you?

_____
_____
_____
_____
_____
_____
_____
_____

What has fear taught you?

_____
_____
_____
_____
_____
_____
_____
_____

5

Dying

As I leave yoga class, Sam tells me she is pregnant, again. There is a desperation, a gripping, to these words. She wants it too much. We share an overly pleasant goodbye and I wish her luck and once I close the car door behind me, I begin to cry.

One night a few months later, Sam comes into the studio to take my class. I notice right away that her belly has not grown; there is no more talk of the baby on the way. I had planned that the focus of the class would be on one central visualization: how our spine begins to form in the womb. Shit.

I have a decision to make. I can do something different entirely or go with what I planned. Changing it feels like cowardice, a way to let both Sam and myself off the hook from what could be an essential practice. Even though I am scared of pushing her too far, I commit.

During the class, I know she is crying. There are long moments where she just lays there, completely lifeless. It's as though she is dead. I leave her alone. You have to die first, to come back to life.

Reflections

What has death taught you?

_____

_____

_____

_____

_____

_____

_____

How has profound sadness cleansed you?

_____

_____

_____

_____

_____

_____

_____

6

Trying

She's looking at me. I've never seen her before in my life but in this class, in this moment, the blonde girl in the pink tank top and black tights is watching me. Each time I look behind me in down dog, she is looking. She thinks I know what I'm doing. And I do. Kind of.

But the truth is

I'm just a woman

In a yoga class

Occasionally looking at my stomach in the mirror

Trying to love myself.

Reflections

What do you see when you look in the mirror?

_____

_____

_____

_____

_____

_____

_____

How is your persona different from who you feel
you are inside?

_____

_____

_____

_____

_____

_____

_____

Acknowledgments

It is entirely possible that these stories would never have seen the light of day without the encouragement of my colleagues Steve Parlato and Julia Petitfrere. These two souls have taught me what love is and nothing less.

I also want to thank my family: my parents, Dean and Joan Marchessault for their encouragement and support, as well as my sister, Anne Marchessault, for her friendship and always-sweet words, and finally for the spiritual guidance of my grandparents, from this world and the next.

I'm so thankful for my first teachers and mentors within the Yoga and Wellness Community: Lisa Crofton, Julie Wallace, and Renee Braunsdorf.

With final appreciation to my partner, Andrew Pelletier, who somehow finds a way to meet me where I am.

About the Author

Kate Pelletier is a community college professor, yoga and meditation teacher, mentor, writer, sacred space holder, and free spirit. You can follow her on Instagram @littlewaveyoga.

This is her first book.